D0490050

VEGETARIAN

OVER 100 SENSATIONAL RECIPES FOR VEGETARIAN MEALS

Simple & Delicious

VEGETARIAN

OVER 100 SENSATIONAL RECIPES FOR VEGETARIAN MEALS

This edition published in 2012
LOVE FOOD is an imprint of Parragon Books Ltd

Parragon
Chartist House
15–17 Trim Street
Bath, BA1 1HA, UK

Copyright © Parragon Books Ltd 2007

LOVE FOOD and the accompanying heart device is a registered trade mark of Parragon Books Ltd in Australia, the UK, USA, India and the EU.

www.parragon.com/lovefood

All rights reserved. No part of this publication may be reproduced, stored in a retrieval system or transmitted, in any form or by any means, electronic, mechanical, photocopying, recording or otherwise, without the prior permission of the copyright holder.

ISBN: 978-1-78186-778-5

Printed in China

Cover design by Geoff Borin
Additional photography by Clive Bozzard Hill
Home economy by Val Barrett and Carol Tennant
Introduction by Anne Sheasby

Notes for the Reader
This book uses both metric and imperial measurements. Follow the same units of measurement throughout; do not mix metric and imperial. All spoon measurements are level: teaspoons are assumed to be 5 ml, and tablespoons are assumed to be 15 ml. Unless otherwise stated, milk is assumed to be full fat, eggs and individual vegetables are medium, and pepper is freshly ground black pepper. Unless otherwise stated, all root vegetables should be washed in plain water and peeled prior to using.

For best results, use a food thermometer when cooking meat and poultry – check the latest government guidelines for current advice.

Garnishes, decorations and serving suggestions are all optional and not necessarily included in the recipe ingredients or method.

The times given are an approximate guide only. Preparation times differ according to the techniques used by different people and the cooking times may also vary from those given. Optional ingredients, variations or serving suggestions have not been included in the time calculations.

Recipes using raw or very lightly cooked eggs should be avoided by infants, the elderly, pregnant women, convalescents and anyone suffering from an illness. Pregnant and breastfeeding women are advised to avoid eating peanuts and peanut products. Sufferers from nut allergies should be aware that some of the ready-made ingredients used in the recipes in this book may contain nuts. Always check the packaging before use.

Vegetarians should be aware that some of the ready-made ingredients used in the recipes in this book may contain animal products. Always check the packaging before use.

Contents

Introduction

In many countries around the world, vegetarianism has been a way of life for centuries. People choose to be vegetarian for numerous different reasons, be it on religious or moral grounds, for health reasons and so on.

The UK Vegetarian Society defines a vegetarian as 'someone living on a diet of grains, pulses, nuts, seeds, vegetables and fruits with or without the use of dairy products and eggs (preferably free-range)'. 'A vegetarian does not eat any meat, poultry, game, fish, shellfish or crustacea, or slaughter by-products such as gelatine or animal fats.'

Different Types of Vegetarian Diets

There are several different kinds of vegetarian diets. Lacto-ovo-vegetarians, the most common type of vegetarians, avoid meat, poultry, fish, etc, but they do eat both dairy products and eggs. Lacto-vegetarians avoid meat, poultry, fish, etc, as well as eggs, but they do eat dairy products. Vegans do not eat meat, poultry and fish, etc, nor dairy products, eggs or any other animal product. Fruitarians and those following a macrobiotic diet also come under the umbrella of vegetarian diets and these eating plans are even more restrictive.

Vegetarian Diet & Health

A typical vegetarian diet is generally a healthy way of eating as it tends to be naturally low in saturated fat (as long as not too much cheese is eaten), and high in dietary fibre and starchy carbohydrate foods. A vegetarian diet includes a wide range of foods such as beans and pulses, cereals and grains, nuts and seeds, fruit, vegetables, dairy foods, soya products and eggs (depending on the type of vegetarian diet). Following a balanced, healthy vegetarian eating plan, and including some foods from each group every day, should provide vegetarians with the correct balance of foods and all the nutrients, vitamins and minerals that they need to keep healthy.

Vegetables and fruit play an important role in vegetarian cooking, adding not only vibrant colours and varied textures and flavours, but also vital vitamins and minerals (such as vitamins A, C and E, iron, zinc and other trace elements), dietary fibre and cancer-protecting antioxidant nutrients.

A wide range of beans and pulses are readily available (either dried or canned), as well as cereals and grains such as pasta (both fresh and dried), rice, bulgur wheat, cornmeal, couscous, quinoa, etc, all of which form the basis of many tempting vegetarian dishes and provide complex carbohydrates, dietary fibre, vitamins and minerals, and some provide a valuable source of protein too.

Nuts and seeds are an ideal way to increase the texture and taste of many recipes whilst adding important nutrients too. Dairy foods, eggs and soya products provide essential protein needed for the growth and repair of all body cells.

Vegetarian Cooking

Successful vegetarian cooking can be achieved by combining the wide variety of foods and ingredients available, to create exciting and tempting dishes from all corners of the globe. Vegetarian cooking doesn't need to be complicated. Quite often the simpler the dish and the less preparation and cooking involved, the better, especially when using fresh produce such as vegetables.

The versatility of many vegetables, not forgetting the humble potato, which is one of the most versatile of all vegetables, means that they lend themselves to creativity in the kitchen. Fresh herbs and spices are also a great way of adding flavour and interest to dishes.

Try experimenting with different ingredients and foods that perhaps you haven't tried before. For example, combine protein-packed beans or pulses with a selection of fresh, colourful vegetables to create a rich, warming winter stew or a light and refreshing summer salad.

This cookbook will introduce you to a tempting selection of delicious and nutritious vegetarian recipes, many of which are quick and easy to make, and all of which will inspire you to create and enjoy vegetarian dishes.

The recipes are presented in four different chapters including Soups & Starters, Snacks & Light Meals, Main Dishes and Side Dishes, offering an extensive choice of enticing recipes for all the family to enjoy.

Soups & Starters

Vegetable & Corn Chowder

serves 4

1 tbsp vegetable oil

1 red onion, diced

1 red pepper, deseeded and diced

3 garlic cloves, crushed

300 g/10 oz potatoes, diced

2 tbsp plain flour

600 ml/1 pint milk

300 ml/½ pint vegetable stock

50 g/2 oz broccoli florets

300 g/10 oz canned sweetcorn, drained

75 g/2¾ oz Cheddar-style vegetarian cheese, grated

salt and pepper

Heat the oil in a large saucepan. Add the onion, red pepper, garlic and potatoes and sauté over a low heat, stirring frequently, for 2–3 minutes.

Stir in the flour and cook, stirring, for 30 seconds. Gradually stir in the milk and stock.

Add the broccoli and sweetcorn. Bring the mixture to the boil, stirring constantly, then reduce the heat and simmer for about 20 minutes, or until all the vegetables are tender.

Stir in 50 g/1¾ oz of the cheese until it melts.

Season to taste and ladle into warmed bowls. Garnish with the remaining cheese and serve.

Creamy Tomato & Basil Soup

serves 6

25 g/1 oz butter

1 tbsp olive oil

1 onion, finely chopped

1 garlic clove, chopped

900 g/2 lb plum tomatoes, chopped

700 ml/1¼ pints vegetable stock

125 ml/4 fl oz dry white wine

2 tbsp sun-dried tomato purée

2 tbsp torn fresh basil leaves

150 ml/5 fl oz double cream

salt and pepper

fresh basil leaves, to garnish

Melt the butter with the oil in a large, heavy-based saucepan. Add the onion and cook, stirring occasionally, for 5 minutes, or until softened. Add the garlic, tomatoes, stock, wine and tomato purée, stir well and season to taste. Partially cover the saucepan and simmer, stirring occasionally, for 20–25 minutes, or until the mixture is soft and pulpy.

Remove the saucepan from the heat, leave to cool slightly, then pour into a blender or food processor. Add the torn basil and process. Push the mixture through a sieve into a clean saucepan with a wooden spoon.

Stir in the cream and reheat the soup, but do not let it boil. Ladle the soup into warmed bowls, garnish with the basil leaves and serve immediately.

Borscht

serves 6

1 onion

55 g/2 oz butter

350 g/12 oz raw beetroot, cut into thin batons, and 1 raw beetroot, grated

1 carrot, cut into thin batons

3 celery sticks, thinly sliced

2 tomatoes, peeled, deseeded and chopped

1.4 litres/2½ pints vegetable stock

1 tbsp white wine vinegar

1 tbsp sugar

2 large fresh dill sprigs

115 g/4 oz white cabbage, shredded

salt and pepper

150 ml/5 fl oz soured cream, to garnish

Slice the onion into rings. Melt the butter in a large, heavy-based saucepan. Add the onion and cook over a low heat, stirring occasionally, for 3–5 minutes, or until softened. Add the beetroot batons, carrot, celery and chopped tomatoes and cook, stirring frequently, for 4–5 minutes.

Add the stock, vinegar, and sugar and snip a tablespoon of dill into the saucepan. Season to taste with salt and pepper. Bring to the boil, reduce the heat and simmer for 35–40 minutes, or until the vegetables are tender.

Stir in the cabbage, cover and simmer for 10 minutes. Stir in the grated beetroot, with any juices, and cook for a further 10 minutes. Ladle into warmed bowls. Garnish with a spoonful of soured cream and another tablespoon of snipped dill and serve.

Carrot & Cumin Soup

serves 4–6

3 tbsp butter or margarine

1 large onion, chopped

1–2 garlic cloves, crushed

350 g/12 oz carrots, sliced

900 ml/1½ pints vegetable stock

¾ tsp ground cumin

2 celery sticks, thinly sliced

115 g/4 oz potato, diced

2 tsp tomato purée

2 tsp lemon juice

2 bay leaves

about 300 ml/½ pint skimmed milk

salt and pepper

celery leaves, to garnish

Melt the butter or margarine in a large pan. Add the onion and garlic and cook very gently until softened.

Add the carrots and cook gently for a further 5 minutes, stirring frequently and taking care they do not brown.

Add the stock, cumin, seasoning, celery, potato, tomato purée, lemon juice and bay leaves and bring to the boil. Cover and simmer for about 30 minutes until the vegetables are tender.

Remove and discard the bay leaves, cool the soup a little and then press it through a sieve or process in a food processor or blender until smooth.

Pour the soup into a clean pan, add the milk and bring to the boil over a low heat. Taste and adjust the seasoning if necessary. Ladle the soup into warmed bowls, garnish each serving with a small celery leaf and serve.

Pepper & Chilli Soup

serves 4

225 g/8 oz red peppers, seeded and sliced

1 onion, sliced

2 garlic cloves, crushed

1 green chilli, chopped

300 ml/½ pint passata

600 ml/1 pint vegetable stock

2 tbsp chopped basil

salt and pepper

basil sprigs, to garnish

Put the sliced red peppers in a large saucepan with the onion, garlic and chilli. Add the passata and the vegetable stock and bring to the boil, stirring well.

Reduce the heat to a simmer and continue to cook the vegetables for 20 minutes, or until the peppers have softened. Drain, reserving the liquid and vegetables separately.

Using the back of a spoon, press the vegetables through a sieve. Alternatively, process in a food processor until smooth.

Return the vegetable purée to a clean saucepan with the reserved cooking liquid. Add the basil, season, and heat through until hot. Garnish the soup with fresh basil sprigs and serve immediately.

Mixed Bean Soup

serves 4

1 onion, chopped

1 garlic clove, finely chopped

2 celery sticks, sliced

1 large carrot, diced

400 g/14 oz canned chopped tomatoes

150 ml/¼ pint dry red wine

1.2 litres/2 pints vegetable stock

1 tsp dried oregano

425 g/15 oz canned mixed beans and pulses, drained

2 courgettes, diced

1 tbsp tomato purée

salt and pepper

shop-bought pesto to garnish

Place the prepared onion, garlic, celery and carrot in a large saucepan. Stir in the tomatoes, red wine, vegetable stock and oregano.

Bring the vegetable mixture to the boil, cover and leave to simmer for 15 minutes. Stir the mixed beans and pulses into the mixture with the courgettes, and continue to cook, uncovered, for a further 5 minutes.

Add the tomato purée to the mixture and season well with salt and pepper to taste. Then heat through, stirring occasionally, for a further 2–3 minutes, but be careful not to allow the mixture to boil again.

Ladle the soup into warm bowls and serve with a spoonful of pesto on each portion.

Lettuce & Rocket Soup

serves 4–6

1 tbsp butter

1 large onion, halved and sliced

2 leeks, sliced

1.5 litres/2¾ pints vegetable stock

85 g/3 oz white rice

2 carrots, thinly sliced

3 garlic cloves

1 bay leaf

2 heads soft round lettuce (about 450 g/1 lb), cored and chopped

175 ml/6 fl oz double cream

freshly grated nutmeg

85 g/3 oz rocket leaves, finely chopped

salt and pepper

rocket leaves, to garnish

Melt the butter in a large saucepan over a medium heat and add the onion and leeks. Cover and cook for 3–4 minutes, stirring frequently, until the vegetables begin to soften.

Add the stock, rice, carrots, garlic and bay leaf with a large pinch of salt. Bring just to the boil. Reduce the heat, cover and simmer for 25–30 minutes, or until the rice and vegetables are tender. Remove the bay leaf.

Add the lettuce to the saucepan and cook for 10 minutes, until the leaves are soft, stirring occasionally.

Allow the soup to cool slightly, then transfer to a blender or a food processor and purée until smooth, working in batches if necessary. (If using a food processor, strain off the cooking liquid and reserve. Purée the soup solids with enough cooking liquid to moisten them, then combine with the remaining liquid.)

Return the soup to the saucepan and place over a low-medium heat. Stir in the cream, reserving a little for the garnish, and the nutmeg. Simmer for 5 minutes, stirring occasionally, until it is reheated.

Add the rocket leaves and simmer for 2–3 minutes, stirring occasionally, until wilted. Adjust the seasoning and ladle the soup into warm bowls. Garnish each serving with a swirl of cream and a rocket leaf, and serve immediately.

Filo-wrapped Asparagus

serves 4

for the dip

85 g/3 oz vegetarian cottage cheese

1 tbsp semi-skimmed milk

4 spring onions, trimmed and finely chopped

2 tbsp chopped fresh mixed herbs, such as basil, mint and tarragon

pepper

for the asparagus

20 asparagus spears

5 sheets filo pastry

lemon wedges, to serve

Preheat the oven to 190°C/375°F/Gas Mark 5. To make the dip, put the cheese in a bowl and add the milk. Beat until smooth then stir in the spring onions, chopped herbs and pepper to taste. Place in a serving bowl, cover lightly and chill in the refrigerator until required.

Cut off and discard the woody end of the asparagus and shave with a vegetable peeler to remove any woody parts from the spears.

Cut the filo pastry into quarters and place one sheet on a work surface. Brush lightly with water then place a spear at one end. Roll up to encase the spear, and place on a large baking sheet. Repeat until all the asparagus spears are wrapped in pastry.

Bake for 10–12 minutes, or until the pastry is golden. Serve the spears with lemon wedges and the dip on the side.

Pepper & Basil Pots

serves 4

1 tsp olive oil

2 shallots, finely chopped

2 garlic cloves, crushed

pepper

2 red peppers, peeled, deseeded and sliced into strips

1 orange pepper, peeled, deseeded and sliced into strips

4 tomatoes, thinly sliced

2 tbsp shredded fresh basil

salad leaves, to serve

Lightly brush 4 ramekin dishes with the oil. Mix the shallots and garlic together in a bowl and season with pepper to taste.

Layer the red and orange peppers with the tomatoes in the prepared ramekin dishes, sprinkling each layer with the shallot mixture and shredded basil. When all the ingredients have been added, cover lightly with clingfilm or baking paper. Weigh down using small weights and leave in the refrigerator for at least 6 hours, or preferably overnight.

When ready to serve, remove the weights and carefully run a knife around the edges. Invert onto serving plates and serve with salad leaves.

Mushroom Pâté

serves 4

15 g/½ oz dried porcini mushrooms

1 tsp olive oil

2 shallots, finely chopped

2 garlic cloves, crushed

1 fresh jalapeño chilli, deseeded and finely chopped

2 celery sticks, trimmed and finely chopped

225 g/8 oz closed cup mushrooms, wiped and sliced

grated rind and juice of 1 orange

25 g/1 oz fresh breadcrumbs

1 tbsp chopped fresh parsley

1 small egg, beaten

pepper

raw vegetables sticks and crisp breads, to serve

Preheat the oven to 180°C/350°F/Gas Mark 4. Put the dried mushrooms in a bowl and cover with almost boiling water. Leave to soak for 30 minutes then drain, chop and reserve.

Heat the oil in a medium heavy-based saucepan, then add the shallots, garlic, chilli and celery. Cook, stirring frequently for 3 minutes, then add both the dried and fresh mushrooms and cook for a further 2 minutes.

Add the orange juice and continue to cook for 3–4 minutes, or until the mushrooms have collapsed. Remove the pan from the heat and stir in the orange rind, breadcrumbs, parsley, beaten egg and pepper to taste. Mix well.

Spoon the mixture into 4 individual ramekin dishes and level the surfaces. Place the dishes in a small baking tin and pour enough water to come halfway up the sides of the ramekins.

Bake for 15–20 minutes, or until a skewer inserted in the centre of each ramekin comes out clean. Remove and either leave to stand for 10 minutes before serving warm or chill until ready to serve. Turn out and serve with vegetable sticks and crisp breads.

Stuffed Aubergine Slices

serves 4

1 medium aubergine

4 tbsp extra virgin olive oil

115 g/4 oz mozzarella-style vegetarian cheese, grated

1 tbsp fresh chopped basil

400 g/14 oz canned tomatoes with added herbs, heated through

extra basil leaves, to garnish

Preheat the oven to 200°C/400°F/Gas Mark 6.

Slice the aubergine lengthways into 8 slices. Brush the slices with oil and place on an ovenproof tray. Bake for 10 minutes, without letting them get too floppy. Remove from the oven. Scatter the grated cheese and basil over the aubergine slices.

Roll up each slice and place the slices in a single layer in a shallow ovenproof dish. Pour over the chopped tomatoes and cook in the oven for 10 minutes or until the sauce bubbles and the cheese melts.

Remove the stuffed aubergine slices from the oven and transfer carefully to serving plates. Spoon any remaining chopped tomatoes on or around the aubergine slices. Garnish with basil leaves and serve while still hot.

Quesadillas

serves 4

4 tbsp finely chopped fresh jalapeño chillies

1 onion, chopped

1 tbsp red wine vinegar

5 tbsp extra virgin olive oil

300–400 g/10½–14 oz canned sweetcorn

8 soft flour tortillas

Put the chillies, onion, vinegar and 4 tablespoons of olive oil in a food processor or blender and process until finely chopped.

Tip into a bowl and stir in the sweetcorn.

Heat the remaining oil in a frying pan, add a tortilla and cook for 1 minute until golden.

Spread a quarter of the chilli mixture over the tortilla and fold over.

Cook for 2–3 minutes until golden and the filling is heated through. Remove from the pan and keep warm. Repeat with the other tortillas and filling. Serve immediately.

Creamed Mushrooms

serves 4

juice of 1 small lemon

450 g/1 lb small button mushrooms

25 g/1 oz butter

1 tbsp sunflower or olive oil

1 small onion, finely chopped

125 ml/4 fl oz whipping or double cream

1 tbsp chopped fresh parsley, plus 4 sprigs, to garnish

salt and pepper

Sprinkle a little of the lemon juice over the mushrooms.

Heat the butter and oil in a frying pan, add the onion and cook for 1 minute. Add the mushrooms, shaking the pan so they do not stick.

Season to taste with salt and pepper, then stir in the cream, chopped parsley and remaining lemon juice.

Heat until hot but do not allow to boil then transfer to a serving plate and garnish with the parsley sprigs.
Serve immediately.

Vegetable Tartlets

makes 12 tartlets

butter, for greasing

12 ready-baked puff pastry cases

2 tbsp olive oil

1 red pepper, deseeded and diced

1 garlic clove, crushed

1 small onion, finely chopped

225 g/8 oz ripe tomatoes, chopped

1 tbsp torn fresh basil

1 tsp fresh or dried thyme

salt and pepper

green salad, to serve

Preheat the oven to 200°C/400°F/Gas Mark 6 and grease several baking trays.

Place the ready-baked pastry cases on the prepared baking trays.

Heat the oil in a frying pan, add the pepper, garlic and onion and cook over a high heat for about 3 minutes until soft.

Add the tomatoes, herbs and seasoning and spoon onto the pastry cases.

Bake for about 5 minutes, or until the filling is piping hot. Serve warm with a green salad.

Aubergine Pâté

serves 4–6

2 large aubergines

4 tbsp extra virgin olive oil

2 garlic cloves, very finely chopped

4 tbsp lemon juice

salt and pepper

6 crisp breads, to serve

Preheat the oven to 180°C/350°F/Gas Mark 4. Score the skins of the aubergines with the point of a sharp knife, without piercing the flesh, and place them on a baking sheet. Bake for 1¼ hours, or until soft.

Remove the aubergines from the oven and leave until cool enough to handle. Cut them in half and, using a spoon, scoop out the flesh into a bowl. Mash the flesh thoroughly.

Gradually beat in the olive oil then stir in the garlic and lemon juice. Season to taste with salt and pepper. Cover with clingfilm and store in the refrigerator until required. Serve with the crisp breads.

Tomato Bruschetta

serves 4

8 slices of rustic bread

4 garlic cloves, halved

8 plum tomatoes, peeled
and diced

extra virgin olive oil,
for drizzling

salt and pepper

fresh basil leaves,
to garnish

Preheat the grill. Lightly toast the bread on both sides. Rub each piece of toast with half a garlic clove and then return to the grill for a few seconds.

Divide the diced tomatoes among the toasts. Season to taste with salt and pepper and drizzle with olive oil. Serve immediately, garnished with basil leaves.

Spring Rolls

serves 12

2 spring onions, plus a few more to garnish

5 dried Chinese mushrooms or fresh open-cap mushrooms

1 large carrot

55 g/2 oz canned bamboo shoots

55 g/2 oz Chinese leaves

2 tbsp vegetable oil, plus extra for deep-frying

225 g/8 oz beansprouts

1 tbsp soy sauce

12 spring roll wrappers

1 egg, beaten

salt

To make the garnish, make several cuts into the stem of each spring onion and place in a bowl of iced water until the tassels open out.

Place the mushrooms in a small bowl and cover with warm water. Leave to soak for 20–25 minutes, then drain and squeeze out the excess water. Remove the tough centres and slice the mushroom caps thinly. Cut the carrot and bamboo shoots into very thin julienne strips. Chop the 2 spring onions and shred the Chinese leaves.

Heat 2 tablespoons of oil in a preheated wok. Add the mushrooms, carrot and bamboo shoots and stir-fry for 2 minutes. Add the spring onions, Chinese leaves, beansprouts and soy sauce. Season to taste with salt and stir-fry for 2 minutes. Cool.

Divide the mixture into 12 equal portions and place one portion on the edge of each spring roll wrapper. Fold in the sides and roll each one up, brushing the join with beaten egg to seal. Heat the oil for deep-frying in a large, heavy-based saucepan to 180–190°C/350–375°F, or until a cube of bread browns in 30 seconds. Add the spring rolls, in batches, and cook for 4–5 minutes, or until golden and crispy. Take care that the oil is not too hot or the rolls will brown on the outside before cooking on the inside. Drain on kitchen paper. Keep warm. Garnish with spring onion tassels and serve.

Hot Garlic-stuffed Mushrooms

serves 4

4 large field mushrooms

4 sprays olive oil

2–3 garlic cloves, crushed

2 shallots

25 g/1 oz fresh wholemeal breadcrumbs

few fresh basil sprigs, plus extra to garnish

25 g/1 oz ready-to-eat dried apricots, chopped

1 tbsp pine kernels

55 g/2 oz feta-style vegetarian cheese

pepper

Preheat the oven to 180°C/350°F/Gas Mark 4. Remove the stalks from the mushrooms and set aside. Spray the bases of the mushrooms with the oil and place undersides up in a roasting tin.

Put the mushroom stalks in a food processor with the garlic, shallots and breadcrumbs. Reserve a few basil sprigs for the garnish then place the remainder in the food processor with the apricots, pine kernels and the cheese. Add pepper to taste.

Process for 1–2 minutes, or until a stuffing consistency is formed, then divide among the mushroom caps.

Bake for 10–12 minutes, or until the mushrooms are tender and the stuffing is crisp on the top. Serve garnished with the reserved basil sprigs.

Snacks & Light Meals

Red Onion, Tomato & Herb Salad

serves 4

900 g/2 lb tomatoes, sliced thinly

1 tbsp sugar (optional)

1 red onion, sliced thinly

large handful coarsely chopped fresh herbs

salt and pepper

for the dressing

2–4 tbsp vegetable oil

2 tbsp red wine vinegar or fruit vinegar

Arrange the tomato slices in a shallow bowl. Sprinkle with sugar (if using), salt and pepper.

Separate the onion slices into rings and scatter over the tomatoes. Sprinkle the herbs over the top. Anything that is in season can be used – for example, tarragon, sorrel, coriander or basil.

Place the dressing ingredients in a jar with a screw-top lid. Shake well. Pour the dressing over the salad and mix gently.

Cover with clingfilm and refrigerate for 20 minutes. Remove the salad from the refrigerator 5 minutes before serving, unwrap the dish and stir gently before setting out on the table.

Potato, Leek & Feta Patties

serves 4

1 whole garlic bulb

115 g/4 oz sweet potatoes, peeled and cut into chunks

175 g/6 oz carrots, peeled and chopped

115 g/4 oz leeks, trimmed and finely chopped

55 g/2 oz feta-style vegetarian cheese, crumbled

1–2 tsp Tabasco sauce, or to taste

1 tbsp chopped fresh coriander

pepper

fresh herbs or salad, to garnish

tomato ketchup, to serve (optional)

Preheat the oven to 190°C/375°F/Gas Mark 5. Break the garlic bulb open, place in a small roasting tin and roast for 20 minutes, or until soft. Remove and when cool enough to handle, squeeze out the roasted garlic flesh.

Cook the sweet potatoes and carrots in a large saucepan of boiling water for 15 minutes, or until soft. Drain and mash then mix in the roasted garlic flesh.

Add the leeks, cheese, Tabasco sauce, coriander and pepper to the sweet potato mixture. Cover and leave to chill in the refrigerator for at least 30 minutes.

Using slightly dampened hands, shape the sweet potato mixture into 8 small round patties and place on a non-stick baking sheet. Bake for 15–20 minutes, or until piping hot. Garnish with fresh herbs or salad and serve with tomato ketchup, if using.

Courgette, Carrot & Tomato Frittata

serves 4

2 sprays olive oil

1 onion, cut into small wedges

1–2 garlic cloves, crushed

2 eggs

2 egg whites

1 courgette, about 85 g/ 3 oz, trimmed and grated

2 carrots, about 115 g/4 oz, peeled and grated

2 tomatoes, chopped

pepper

1 tbsp shredded fresh basil, for sprinkling

Heat the oil in a large non-stick frying pan, add the onion and garlic and sauté for 5 minutes, stirring frequently. Beat the eggs and egg whites together in a bowl then pour into the pan. Using a spatula or fork, pull the egg mixture from the sides of the pan into the centre, allowing the uncooked egg to take its place.

Once the base has set lightly, add the grated courgette and carrots with the tomatoes. Add pepper to taste and continue to cook over a low heat until the eggs are set to personal preference.

Sprinkle with the shredded basil, cut the frittata into quarters and serve.

Spicy Stuffed Peppers

serves 4

4 assorted coloured peppers

3 sprays olive oil

1 onion, finely chopped

2 garlic cloves, chopped

2.5-cm/1-inch piece fresh root ginger, peeled and grated

1–2 fresh serrano chillies, deseeded and chopped

1 tsp ground cumin

1 tsp ground coriander

85 g/3 oz cooked brown basmati rice

1 large carrot, about 115 g/ 4 oz, peeled and grated

1 large courgette, about 85 g/3 oz, trimmed and grated

25 g/1 oz ready-to-eat dried apricots, finely chopped

1 tbsp chopped fresh coriander

150 ml/5 fl oz water

pepper

fresh herbs, to garnish

Preheat the oven to 190°C/375°F/Gas Mark 5. Cut the tops off the peppers and reserve. Discard the seeds from each pepper. Place the peppers in a large bowl and cover with boiling water. Leave to soak for 10 minutes then drain and reserve.

Heat a non-stick frying pan and spray with the oil. Add the onion, garlic, ginger and chillies and sauté for 3 minutes, stirring frequently. Sprinkle in the ground spices and continue to cook for a further 2 minutes.

Remove the pan from the heat and stir in the rice, carrot, courgette, apricots, chopped coriander, and pepper to taste. Stir well, then use to stuff the peppers.

Place the stuffed peppers in an ovenproof dish large enough to allow the peppers to stand upright. Put the reserved tops in position. Pour the water around their bases, cover loosely with the lid or foil and bake for 25–30 minutes, or until piping hot. Serve garnished with herbs.

Tomato Ratatouille

serves 4

4 sprays olive oil

1 onion, cut into small wedges

2–4 garlic cloves, chopped

1 small aubergine, trimmed and chopped

1 small red pepper, deseeded and chopped

1 small yellow pepper, deseeded and chopped

1 courgette, trimmed and chopped

2 tbsp tomato purée

3 tbsp water

115 g/4 oz mushrooms, sliced if large

225 g/8 oz ripe tomatoes, chopped

pepper

1 tbsp shredded fresh basil, to garnish

25 g/1 oz Parmesan-style vegetarian cheese, freshly shaved, to serve

Heat the oil in a heavy-based saucepan, add the onion, garlic and aubergine and cook, stirring frequently for 3 minutes.

Add the peppers and courgette. Mix the tomato purée and water together in a small bowl and stir into the pan. Bring to the boil, cover with a lid, reduce the heat to a simmer and cook for 10 minutes.

Add the mushrooms and chopped tomatoes with pepper to taste and continue to simmer for 12–15 minutes, stirring occasionally, until the vegetables are tender.

Divide the ratatouille between 4 warmed bowls, garnish each with shredded basil and serve with freshly shaved Parmesan-style vegetarian cheese to sprinkle over.

Open Rösti Omelette

serves 4

55 g/2 oz old potatoes, peeled and grated

1 onion, grated

2 garlic cloves, crushed

1 carrot, about 115 g/4 oz, peeled and grated

4 sprays olive oil

1 yellow pepper, peeled and thinly sliced

1 courgette, about 85 g/ 3 oz, trimmed and thinly sliced

85 g/3 oz cherry tomatoes, halved

2 eggs

3 egg whites

1 tbsp snipped fresh chives

pepper

fresh rocket, to garnish

Put the grated potatoes into a large bowl and cover with cold water. Leave for 15 minutes then drain, rinse thoroughly and dry on absorbent kitchen paper or a clean tea towel. Mix with the grated onion, garlic and carrot.

Heat a heavy-based non-stick frying pan and spray with the oil. Add the potato, onion, garlic and carrot mixture and cook over a low heat for 5 minutes, pressing the vegetables down firmly with a spatula. Add the peeled pepper and courgette slices. Cover with a lid or crumpled piece of foil and cook very gently, stirring occasionally, for 5 minutes.

Add the halved cherry tomatoes and cook for a further 2 minutes, or until the vegetables are tender.

Beat the whole eggs, egg whites, pepper to taste and the chives together in a bowl. Pour over the vegetable mixture and cook for 4–5 minutes, stirring the egg from the sides of the pan towards the centre, until the vegetables are tender and the eggs are set. Serve immediately, garnished with rocket leaves.

French Bean & Walnut Salad

serves 2

450 g/1 lb French beans

1 small onion, finely chopped

1 garlic clove, chopped

4 tbsp freshly grated Parmesan-style vegetarian cheese

2 tbsp chopped walnuts or almonds, to garnish

for the dressing

3 tbsp extra virgin olive oil

2 tbsp white wine vinegar

salt and pepper

2 tsp chopped fresh tarragon

Top and tail the beans, but leave them whole. Cook for 3–4 minutes in salted boiling water. Drain well, run under the cold tap to refresh and drain again. Put into a mixing bowl and add the onion, garlic and cheese.

Place the dressing ingredients in a jar with a screw-top lid. Shake well. Pour the dressing over the salad and toss gently to coat. Cover with clingfilm and chill for at least 30 minutes.

Remove the beans from the refrigerator 10 minutes before serving. Give them a quick stir and transfer to an attractive, shallow serving dish.

Toast the nuts in a dry frying pan over a medium heat for 2 minutes, or until they begin to brown. Sprinkle the toasted nuts over the beans to garnish before serving.

Cheesy Baked Courgettes

serves 4

4 medium courgettes

2 tbsp extra virgin olive oil

115 g/4 oz mozzarella-style vegetarian cheese, sliced thinly

2 large tomatoes, deseeded and diced

2 tsp fresh basil or oregano, chopped

Preheat the oven to 200°C/400°F/Gas Mark 6.

Slice the courgettes lengthways into 4 strips each. Brush with oil and place on an ovenproof tray.

Bake the courgettes in the oven for 10 minutes without letting them get too floppy.

Remove the courgettes from the oven. Arrange slices of cheese on top and sprinkle with diced tomato and basil or oregano. Return to the oven for 5 minutes or until the cheese melts.

Remove the courgettes from the oven and transfer carefully to serving plates, or serve straight from the baking dish.

Nutty Beetroot Salad

serves 4

3 tbsp red wine vinegar or fruit vinegar

3 cooked beetroot, grated

2 tart apples, eg Granny Smith

2 tbsp lemon juice

4 large handfuls mixed salad leaves

4 tbsp pecans

for the dressing

50 ml/2 fl oz plain yoghurt

50 ml/2 fl oz mayonnaise

1 garlic clove, chopped

1 tbsp chopped fresh dill

salt and pepper

Sprinkle vinegar over the beetroot, cover with clingfilm and chill for at least 4 hours.

Core and slice the apples, place the slices in a dish and sprinkle with the lemon juice.

Combine the dressing ingredients in a small bowl. Remove the beetroot from the refrigerator and dress. Add the apples to the beetroot and mix gently to coat with the salad dressing.

To serve, arrange a handful of salad leaves on each plate and top with a large spoonful of the apple and beetroot mixture.

Toast the pecans in a dry frying pan over a medium heat for 2 minutes, or until they begin to brown. Sprinkle over the beetroot and apple to garnish.

Tomato & Feta Salad

serves 4

1 kg/2 lb 4 oz ripe
tomatoes, thickly sliced

225 g/8 oz feta-style
vegetarian cheese

125 ml/4 fl oz extra virgin
olive oil

16 black olives, stoned

pepper

Arrange the tomato slices in concentric rings on a serving dish. Crumble the cheese over the tomatoes and drizzle with the olive oil. Top with the olives.

Season to taste with pepper. Salt is probably not necessary because feta is already quite salty. Leave to stand for 30 minutes before serving.

Goat's Cheese Tarts

makes about 12 tarts

butter, for greasing

400 g/14 oz packet ready-rolled puff pastry

1 tbsp plain flour

1 egg, beaten

3 tbsp onion or tomato relish

three x 115-g/4-oz vegetarian goat's cheese logs, sliced

extra virgin olive oil, for drizzling

pepper

Preheat the oven to 200°C/400°F/Gas Mark 6 and grease several baking trays.

Cut out as many 7.5-cm/3-inch rounds as possible from the pastry on a lightly floured work surface.

Place the rounds on the baking trays and press gently about 2.5 cm/1 inch from the edge of each with a smaller 5-cm/2-inch pastry cutter.

Brush the rounds with beaten egg and prick with a fork.

Top each circle with a little relish and a slice of cheese. Drizzle with oil and sprinkle over a little black pepper.

Bake for 8–10 minutes, or until the pastry is crisp and the cheese is bubbling. Serve warm.

Falafel Burgers

serves 4

two x 400-g/14-oz cans chickpeas, drained and rinsed

1 small onion, chopped

zest and juice of 1 lime

2 tsp ground coriander

2 tsp ground cumin

6 tbsp plain flour

4 tbsp olive oil

4 sprigs fresh basil, to garnish

tomato salsa, to serve

Put the chickpeas, onion, lime zest and juice and the spices into a food processor and process to a coarse paste.

Tip the mixture out onto a clean work surface or chopping board and shape into 4 patties.

Spread the flour out on a large flat plate and use to coat the patties.

Heat the oil in a large frying pan, add the burgers and cook for 2 minutes on each side until crisp. Garnish with basil and serve with tomato salsa.

Wilted Spinach, Yogurt & Walnut Salad

serves 2

450 g/1 lb fresh spinach leaves

1 onion, chopped

1 tbsp olive oil

225 ml/8 fl oz natural yogurt

1 garlic clove, finely chopped

2 tbsp chopped toasted walnuts

2–3 tsp chopped fresh mint

salt and pepper

pitta bread, to serve

Put the spinach and onion into a saucepan, cover and cook gently for a few minutes until the spinach has wilted.

Add the oil and cook for a further 5 minutes. Season to taste with salt and pepper.

Combine the yogurt and garlic in a bowl.

Put the spinach and onion into a serving bowl and pour over the yogurt mixture. Scatter over the walnuts and chopped mint and serve with pitta bread.

Baked Chilli Cheese Sandwiches

makes 4 sandwiches

350 g/12 oz Cheddar-style vegetarian cheese

115 g/4 oz butter, softened, plus extra to finish

4 fresh green chillies, deseeded and chopped

½ tsp ground cumin

8 thick slices bread

Preheat the oven to 190°C/375°F/Gas Mark 5. Mix the cheese and butter together in a bowl until creamy then add the chillies and cumin.

Spread this mixture over 4 slices of bread and top with the remaining slices.

Spread the outside of the sandwiches with extra butter and bake for 8–10 minutes until crisp. Serve.

Grilled Halloumi with Herbed Couscous

serves 4

450 g/1 lb halloumi-style vegetarian cheese, cut into 5-mm/¼-inch slices

4 tbsp chilli oil

for the herbed couscous

400 ml/14 fl oz hot vegetable stock

225 g/8 oz couscous

2 tbsp chopped fresh mixed herbs

2 tsp lemon juice

1 tbsp olive oil

Preheat the grill to high and line the grill rack with foil.

Put the cheese slices in a bowl, pour over the chilli oil and toss well to coat the cheese.

Place the cheese on the grill rack and cook under the grill for 2–3 minutes on each side until golden.

Meanwhile, stir the hot stock into the couscous in a large bowl. Cover and leave to stand for 5 minutes.

Stir the herbs, lemon juice and olive oil into the couscous. Serve with the grilled halloumi-style vegetarian cheese.

Nachos with Chillies & Olives

serves 4

1 kg/2 lb 4 oz tortilla chips

6 tbsp chopped pickled jalapeño chillies

115 g/4 oz black olives, stoned and sliced

450 g/1 lb Cheddar-style vegetarian cheese, grated

dipping sauce

Preheat the oven to 180°C/350°F/Gas Mark 4. Spread out the tortilla chips in a large ovenproof dish.

Sprinkle the chillies, olives and grated cheese evenly over the tortilla chips and bake for 12–15 minutes, or until the cheese is melted and bubbling. Serve immediately with a dipping sauce of your choice.

Warm Goat's Cheese Salad

serves 4

1 small iceberg lettuce, torn into pieces

handful of rocket leaves

few radicchio leaves, torn

6 slices French bread

115 g/4 oz vegetarian goat's cheese, sliced

for the dressing

4 tbsp extra virgin olive oil

1 tbsp white wine vinegar

salt and pepper

Preheat the grill. Divide all the leaves between 4 individual salad bowls.

Toast one side of the bread under the grill until golden. Place a slice of cheese on top of each untoasted side and toast until the cheese is just melting.

Put all the dressing ingredients into a bowl and beat together until combined. Pour over the leaves, tossing to coat.

Cut each slice of bread in half and place 3 halves on top of each salad. Toss very gently to combine and serve warm.

Moroccan Tomato & Red Pepper Salad

serves 4

3 red peppers

4 ripe tomatoes

½ bunch of fresh coriander, chopped

2 garlic cloves, finely chopped

salt and pepper

Preheat the grill. Place the peppers on a baking sheet and cook under the grill, turning occasionally, for 15 minutes. Add the tomatoes and grill, turning occasionally, for a further 5–10 minutes, or until all the skins are charred and blistered. Remove from the heat and leave to cool.

Peel and deseed the peppers and tomatoes and slice the flesh thinly. Place in a bowl, mix well and season with salt and pepper. Sprinkle with the coriander and garlic, cover with clingfilm and chill in the refrigerator for at least 1 hour. Just before serving, drain off any excess liquid.

Main
Dishes

Chilli Broccoli Pasta

serves 4

225 g/8 oz dry penne or macaroni

225 g/8 oz broccoli

50 ml/2 fl oz extra virgin olive oil

2 large garlic cloves, chopped

2 fresh red chillies, deseeded and diced

8 cherry tomatoes (optional)

small handful of fresh basil or parsley, to garnish

salt

Cook the penne or other pasta in a large pan of salted boiling water for about 10 minutes, until tender but still firm to the bite. Remove from the heat, drain, rinse with cold water and drain again. Set aside.

Cut the broccoli into florets and cook in salted boiling water for 5 minutes. Drain, rinse with cold water and drain again.

Heat the olive oil in the pan that the pasta was cooked in. Add the garlic, chillies and tomatoes, if using. Cook over a high heat for 1 minute.

Return the broccoli to the pan with the oil and mix well. Cook for 2 minutes to heat through. Add the pasta and mix well again. Cook for 1 minute longer.

Remove the pasta from the heat, turn into a large serving bowl and serve garnished with basil or parsley.

Mushroom & Cauliflower Cheese Crumble

serves 4

1 medium cauliflower

55 g/2 oz butter

115 g/4 oz button mushrooms, sliced

salt and pepper

for the topping

115 g/4 oz dry breadcrumbs

2 tbsp grated Parmesan-style vegetarian cheese

1 tsp dried oregano

1 tsp dried parsley

2 tbsp butter

Bring a large pan of salted water to the boil.

Break the cauliflower into small florets and cook in the boiling water for 3 minutes. Remove from the heat, drain well and transfer to a large shallow ovenproof dish.

Preheat the oven to 230°C/450°F/Gas Mark 8. Melt the butter in a small frying pan over a medium heat. Add the sliced mushrooms, stir to coat and cook gently for 3 minutes. Remove from the heat and add to the cauliflower. Season with salt and pepper.

Combine the breadcrumbs, cheese and herbs in a small mixing bowl, then sprinkle the crumbs over the vegetables.

Dice the butter for the topping and dot over the crumbs. Place the dish in the oven and bake for 15 minutes, or until the crumbs are golden brown and crisp. Serve from the cooking dish.

Caramelized Onion Tart

serves 4–6

100 g/3½ oz unsalted butter

600 g/1 lb 5 oz onions, thinly sliced

2 eggs

100 ml/3½ fl oz double cream

100 g/3½ oz grated Gruyère-style vegetarian cheese

20 cm/8 inch baked pastry case

100 g/3½ oz grated Parmesan-style vegetarian cheese

salt and pepper

Melt the butter over a medium heat in a heavy frying pan. Stir in the onions and cook until they are well browned and caramelized. (This will take up to 30 minutes, depending on the width of the pan.) Stir frequently to avoid burning. Remove the onions from the pan and set aside.

Preheat the oven to 190°C/375°F/Gas Mark 5.

Beat the eggs in a large mixing bowl, stir in the cream and season with salt and pepper. Add the Gruyère-style vegetarian cheese and mix well. Mix in the cooked onions.

Pour the egg and onion mixture into the baked pastry case, sprinkle with Parmesan-style vegetarian cheese and place on an ovenproof tray. Bake for 15–20 minutes or until the filling has set and begun to brown.

Remove from the oven and leave to rest for at least 10 minutes. The tart can be served hot or left to cool to room temperature.

Leek & Egg Mornay

serves 4

2 tbsp butter

4 leeks, trimmed and sliced

8 hard-boiled eggs, shelled and quartered

55 g/2 oz butter

55 g/2 oz plain flour

300 ml/10 fl oz milk

55 g/2 oz Cheddar-style or emmenthal-style vegetarian cheese, grated

1 tsp wholegrain mustard

cayenne pepper (optional)

salt and pepper

Melt the butter in a frying pan over medium heat, add the leeks and cook. Remove when soft and add to a baking dish. Arrange the egg quarters on top and season to taste.

Preheat the grill to high.

Meanwhile, melt the butter in a small pan over a medium heat. Gradually add the flour, stirring constantly until it has been absorbed. Still stirring, slowly add the milk, until blended. Bring the sauce to the boil, reduce the heat and simmer, stirring, until it thickens. Add the cheese, mustard and cayenne pepper (if using), stirring until well blended. Pour the sauce over the eggs and leeks.

Put the dish under the grill for 2–3 minutes. Serve when bubbling.

Cheese & Tomato Pizza

serves 4–6

23-cm/9-inch ready-made
thin-crust pizza base
or 1 ciabatta loaf, sliced
horizontally

fresh basil leaves, torn

for the tomato topping

150 ml/5 fl oz tomato
passata

3 tbsp tomato purée

2 garlic cloves, crushed

pinch each of sugar, salt
and pepper

handful of cherry tomatoes

for the cheese topping

150 ml/5 fl oz tomato
passata

3 tbsp tomato purée

115 g/4 oz jar roasted
peppers, drained and
thickly sliced

a few black olives

115 g/4 oz firm mozzarella-
style vegetarian cheese,
grated

55 g/2 oz Parmesan-style
vegetarian cheese, grated

salt and pepper

Preheat the oven to 200°C/400°F/Gas Mark 6. To make the tomato topping, mix the passata, tomato purée, garlic, sugar and salt and pepper together in a bowl. Spread over the ready-made pizza base and scatter with the cherry tomatoes.

To make the cheese topping, mix the tomato passata and tomato purée together in a bowl and spread over the pizza base. Top with the peppers and the olives. Season with salt and pepper and scatter the cheeses over the top.

Bake in the oven for 8–10 minutes until hot and bubbling. Scatter with basil leaves and serve immediately.

Mozzarella Gnocchi

serves 2–4

butter, for greasing

450 g/1 lb packet potato gnocchi

200 ml/7 fl oz double cream

225 g/8 oz firm mozzarella-style vegetarian cheese, grated or chopped

salt and pepper

Preheat the grill and grease a large baking dish.

Cook the gnocchi in a large saucepan of boiling salted water for about 3 minutes, or according to the packet instructions.

Drain and put into the prepared baking dish.

Season the cream with salt and pepper and drizzle over the gnocchi. Scatter over the cheese and cook under the grill for a few minutes until the top is browned and bubbling. Serve immediately.

Bubble & Squeak

serves 4

450 g/1 lb floury potatoes, peeled and diced

2 tbsp milk

55 g/2 oz butter

225 g/8 oz green cabbage, shredded

225 g/8 oz carrots, sliced thinly

1 medium onion, chopped

55 g/2 oz Cheddar-style vegetarian cheese, grated

salt and pepper

Cook the potatoes in salted water for 10 minutes, or until soft. Drain well and turn into a large mixing bowl. Mash until smooth. Beat with the milk, half of the butter and salt and pepper to taste.

Cook the cabbage and carrots separately in salted boiling water for 5 minutes. Drain well. Mix the cabbage into the potatoes. Melt the remaining butter in a small frying pan and cook the onion over a medium heat until soft but not brown.

Preheat the oven to 190°C/375°F/Gas Mark 5.

Spread a layer of mashed potatoes in the bottom of a greased shallow ovenproof dish. Layer onions on top, then carrots. Repeat to use up all the ingredients, finishing with a layer of potato.

Sprinkle the grated cheese on top, place the dish in the oven and bake for 45 minutes, or until the top is golden and crusty. Remove from the oven and serve immediately.

Leek & Spinach Pie

serves 6–8

225 g/8 oz puff pastry

2 tbsp unsalted butter

2 leeks, sliced finely

225 g/8 oz spinach, chopped

2 eggs

300 ml/10 fl oz double cream

pinch of dried thyme

salt and pepper

Roll the pastry into a rectangle about 25 x 30 cm/ 10 x 12 inches. Leave to rest for 5 minutes, then press into a 20 x 25 cm/8 x 10 inch flan dish. Do not trim the overhang. Cover the pastry with aluminium foil and refrigerate.

Preheat the oven to 180°C/350°F/Gas Mark 4.

Melt the butter in a large frying pan over a medium heat. Add the leeks, stir and cook gently for 5 minutes, or until soft. Add the spinach and cook for 3 minutes, or until soft. Leave to cool.

Beat the eggs in a bowl. Stir in the cream and season with thyme, salt and pepper. Remove the pastry case and uncover. Spread the cooked vegetables over the base. Pour in the egg mixture.

Place on a baking sheet and bake for 30 minutes, or until set. Remove the flan from the oven and leave it to rest for 10 minutes before serving. Serve directly from the flan dish.

Tofu Stir-fry

serves 4

2 tbsp sunflower or olive oil

350 g/12 oz firm tofu, cubed

225 g/8 oz pak choi, roughly chopped

1 garlic clove, chopped

4 tbsp sweet chilli sauce

2 tbsp light soy sauce

Heat 1 tablespoon of oil in a wok, add the tofu in batches and stir-fry for 2–3 minutes until golden. Remove and set aside.

Add the pak choi to the wok and stir-fry for a few seconds until tender and wilted. Remove and set aside.

Add the remaining oil to the wok, then add the garlic and stir-fry for 30 seconds.

Stir in the chilli sauce and soy sauce and bring to the boil.

Return the tofu and pak choi to the wok and toss gently until coated in the sauce. Serve immediately.

Creamy Ricotta, Mint & Garlic Pasta

serves 4

300 g/10½ oz short fresh pasta shapes

140 g/5 oz ricotta-style vegetarian cheese

1–2 roasted garlic cloves from a jar, finely chopped

150 ml/5 fl oz double cream

1 tbsp chopped fresh mint and 4 sprigs, to garnish

salt and pepper

Cook the pasta in a large saucepan of boiling salted water for about 3 minutes, or according to the packet instructions until tender but still firm to the bite.

Beat the cheese, garlic, cream and chopped mint together in a bowl until smooth.

Drain the cooked pasta then tip back into the pan. Pour in the cheese mixture and toss together.

Season with pepper and serve immediately, garnished with the sprigs of mint.

Noodle Stir-fry

serves 2

140 g/5 oz flat rice noodles

6 tbsp soy sauce

2 tbsp lemon juice

1 tsp granulated sugar

½ tsp cornflour

1 tbsp vegetable oil

2 tsp grated fresh root ginger

2 garlic cloves, chopped

4–5 spring onions, trimmed and sliced

2 tbsp rice wine or dry sherry

200 g/7 oz canned water chestnuts, sliced

Put the noodles in a large bowl and cover with boiling water. Leave to stand for 4 minutes. Drain and rinse under cold running water.

Mix the soy sauce, lemon juice, sugar and cornflour together in small bowl.

Heat the oil in a wok, add the ginger and garlic and stir-fry for 1 minute.

Add the spring onions and stir-fry for 3 minutes.

Add the rice wine or dry sherry, followed by the soy sauce mixture and cook for 1 minute.

Stir in the water chestnuts and noodles and cook for a further 1–2 minutes, or until heated through. Serve immediately.

Pasta with Olive Sauce

serves 2–4

350 g/12 oz fresh pasta shapes

6 tbsp olive oil

½ tsp freshly grated nutmeg

½ tsp black pepper

1 garlic clove, crushed

2 tbsp tapenade

85g/3 oz black or green olives, stoned and sliced

1 tbsp chopped fresh parsley, to garnish (optional)

salt

Cook the pasta in a large saucepan of boiling salted water for about 4 minutes, or according to the packet instructions until tender but still firm to the bite.

Meanwhile, put ½ teaspoon of salt with the oil, nutmeg, pepper, garlic, tapenade and olives in another saucepan and heat slowly but don't allow to boil. Cover and leave to stand for 3–4 minutes.

Drain the pasta and return to the saucepan. Add the flavoured oil and heat gently for 1–2 minutes. Serve immediately garnished, with chopped parsley, if using.

Vegetable Chilli

serves 4

1 aubergine, cut into 2.5-cm/1-inch slices

1 tbsp olive oil, plus extra for brushing

1 large red onion, chopped finely

2 red or yellow peppers, deseeded and chopped finely

3–4 garlic cloves, finely chopped or crushed

800 g/1 lb 12 oz canned chopped tomatoes

1 tbsp mild chilli powder

½ tsp ground cumin

½ tsp dried oregano

2 small courgettes, quartered lengthways and sliced

400 g/14 oz canned kidney beans, drained and rinsed

450 ml/16 fl oz water

1 tbsp tomato purée

6 spring onions, chopped finely

115 g/4 oz Cheddar-style vegetarian cheese, grated

salt and pepper

Brush the aubergine slices on one side with olive oil. Heat half the oil in a large, heavy-based frying pan over a medium-high heat. Add the aubergine slices, oiled-side up, and cook for 5–6 minutes, or until browned on one side. Turn the slices over, cook on the other side until browned and transfer to a plate. Cut into bite-sized pieces.

Heat the remaining oil in a large saucepan over a medium heat. Add the onion and peppers and cook, stirring occasionally, for 3–4 minutes, or until the onion is just softened, but not browned.

Add the garlic and cook for a further 2–3 minutes, or until the onion is beginning to colour.

Add the tomatoes, chilli powder, cumin and oregano. Season to taste with salt and pepper. Bring just to the boil, reduce the heat, cover and simmer gently for 15 minutes.

Add the courgettes, aubergine pieces and kidney beans. Stir in the water and the tomato purée. Return to the boil, then cover and continue simmering for 45 minutes, or until the vegetables are tender. Taste and adjust the seasoning if necessary. Ladle into warmed serving bowls and top with spring onions and cheese.

Spaghetti with Parsley & Parmesan

serves 4

450 g/1 lb dried spaghetti

175 g/6 oz unsalted butter

4 tbsp chopped fresh
flat-leaf parsley

225 g/8 oz Parmesan-style
vegetarian cheese, grated

salt

Cook the pasta in a large saucepan of boiling salted water for 10–12 minutes, or until tender but still firm to the bite. Drain and tip into a warmed serving dish.

Add the butter, parsley and half the cheese and toss well, using 2 forks, until the butter and cheese have melted. Serve immediately with the remaining cheese handed separately.

Vegetarian Lasagne

serves 4

40 g/1½ oz dried porcini mushrooms

2 tbsp olive oil

1 onion, finely chopped

400 g/14 oz canned chopped tomatoes

55 g/2 oz butter, plus extra for greasing

450 g/1 lb button mushrooms, thinly sliced

1 garlic clove, finely chopped

1 tbsp lemon juice

6 sheets no-precook lasagne

55 g/2 oz freshly grated Parmesan-style vegetarian cheese

salt and peppe

cheese sauce

50 g/1¾ oz butter

50 g/1¾ oz plain flour

600 ml/1 pint milk

100 g/3½ oz Cheddar-style vegetarian cheese, grated

Preheat the oven to 200°C/400°F/Gas Mark 6. Place the porcini mushrooms in a small bowl, cover with boiling water and leave to soak for 30 minutes. Meanwhile, heat the oil in a small frying pan. Add the onion and cook, stirring occasionally, for 5 minutes, or until softened. Add the tomatoes and cook, stirring frequently, for 7–8 minutes. Season with salt and pepper and reserve.

Drain and slice the porcini mushrooms. Melt half the butter in a large, heavy-based frying pan. Add the porcini and button mushrooms and cook until they begin to release their juices. Add the garlic and lemon juice and season to taste with salt and pepper. Cook over a low heat, stirring occasionally, until almost all the liquid has evaporated.

To make the cheese sauce, melt the butter in a saucepan over a low heat. Stir in the flour and cook, stirring constantly, for 2-3 minutes. Gradually add the milk and cook, continuing to stir constantly, until the sauce is thick and smooth. Season to taste with salt and pepper and stir in the Cheddar cheese.

Lightly grease an ovenproof dish with butter. Spread a layer of the cheese sauce over the base of the dish. Place a layer of lasagne sheets on top, cover with the mushrooms, another layer of sauce, another layer of lasagne, the tomato mixture and finally, another layer of sauce. Sprinkle with the Parmesan-style vegetarian cheese and dot with the remaining butter. Bake in the preheated oven for 20 minutes. Leave to stand for 5 minutes before serving.

Cheese & Vegetable Tart

serves 4

350 g/12 oz ready-made shortcrust pastry, thawed if frozen

280 g/10 oz mixed frozen vegetables

150 ml/5 fl oz double cream

115 g/4 oz Cheddar-style vegetarian cheese, grated

salt and pepper

Thinly roll out the dough on a lightly floured work surface and use to line a 23-cm/9-inch quiche tin. Prick the base and chill in the refrigerator for 30 minutes. Preheat the oven to 200°C/400°F/Gas Mark 6.

Line the pastry case with foil and half-fill with baking beans. Place the tin on a baking sheet and bake for 15–20 minutes, or until just firm. Remove the beans and foil, return the pastry case to the oven and bake for a further 5–7 minutes until golden. Remove the pastry case from the oven and leave to cool in the tin.

Meanwhile, cook the frozen vegetables in a saucepan of salted boiling water. Drain and leave to cool.

When ready to cook, preheat the oven again to 200°C/400°F/Gas Mark 6. Mix the cooked vegetables and cream together and season with salt and pepper. Spoon the mixture evenly into the pastry case and sprinkle with the cheese. Bake for 15 minutes, or until the cheese has melted and is turning golden. Serve hot or cold.

Pasta with Tomatoes & Spinach

serves 4

450 g/1 lb dried orecchiette or other pasta shapes

3 tbsp olive oil

225 g/8 oz fresh baby spinach leaves, tough stalks removed

450 g/1 lb cherry tomatoes, halved

Parmesan-style vegetarian cheese, grated (optional)

salt and pepper

Cook the pasta in a large saucepan of boiling salted water for 10–12 minutes, or until tender but still firm to the bite.

Heat the oil in a saucepan, add the spinach and tomatoes and cook, gently stirring occasionally, for 2–3 minutes, or until the spinach has wilted and the tomatoes are heated through but not disintegrating.

Drain the pasta and add it to the pan of vegetables. Toss gently, season with salt and pepper, sprinkle over some cheese, if using, and serve immediately.

Summer Stir-fry

serves 4

115 g/4 oz French beans

115 g/4 oz mangetout

115 g/4 oz carrots

115 g/4 oz asparagus spears

½ red pepper

½ orange pepper

½ yellow pepper

2 celery sticks

3 spring onions

2 tbsp groundnut or sunflower oil

1 tsp finely chopped fresh root ginger

2 garlic cloves, finely chopped

115 g/4 oz broccoli florets

salt

Chinese chives, to garnish

Slice the French beans, mangetout, carrots, asparagus, peppers, celery and spring onions and reserve. Heat half the oil in a preheated wok or heavy-based frying pan. Add the ginger and garlic and stir-fry for a few seconds, then add the French beans and stir-fry for 2 minutes.

Add the mangetout, stir-fry for 1 minute, then add the broccoli florets, carrots and asparagus and stir-fry for 2 minutes.

Add the remaining oil, the peppers, celery and spring onions and stir-fry for a further 2–3 minutes, or until all the vegetables are crisp and tender. Season to taste with salt and serve immediately, garnished with Chinese chives.

Side
Dishes

Roasted Vegetables

serves 4

1 onion, cut into wedges

2–4 garlic cloves, left whole but peeled

1 aubergine, about 225 g/ 8 oz, trimmed and cut into cubes

2 courgettes, about 175 g/ 6 oz, trimmed and cut into chunks

300 g/10½ oz butternut squash, peeled, deseeded and cut into small wedges

2 assorted coloured peppers, deseeded and cut into chunks

2 tsp olive oil

1 tbsp shredded fresh basil

pepper

Preheat the oven to 200°C/400°F/Gas Mark 6. Place the onion wedges, whole garlic cloves and aubergine cubes in a large roasting tin.

Add the courgettes, squash and peppers to the roasting tin then pour over the oil. Turn the vegetables until they are lightly coated in the oil.

Roast the vegetables for 35–40 minutes, or until softened but not mushy. Turn the vegetables over occasionally during cooking.

Remove the vegetables from the oven, season with pepper to taste and stir. Scatter with shredded basil and serve divided between 4 warmed bowls while still warm.

Lemon & Garlic Spinach

serves 4

4 tbsp olive oil

2 garlic cloves, thinly sliced

450 g/1 lb fresh spinach, torn or shredded

juice of ½ lemon

salt and pepper

Heat the olive oil on a high heat in a large frying pan. Add the garlic and spinach and cook, stirring constantly, until the spinach is soft. Take care not to let the spinach burn.

Remove from the heat, turn into a serving bowl and sprinkle with lemon juice. Season with salt and pepper. Mix well and serve either hot or at room temperature.

Mixed Cabbage Coleslaw

serves 4

85 g/3 oz red cabbage

85 g/3 oz hard white cabbage

55 g/2 oz green cabbage

2 carrots, about 175 g/6 oz, peeled and grated

1 white onion, finely sliced

2 red apples, cored and chopped

4 tbsp orange juice

2 celery sticks, trimmed and finely sliced

55 g/2 oz canned sweetcorn kernels

2 tbsp raisins

for the dressing

4 tbsp low fat natural yogurt

1 tbsp chopped fresh parsley

pepper

Discard the outer leaves and hard central core from the cabbages and shred finely. Wash well in plenty of cold water and drain thoroughly.

Place the cabbages in a bowl and stir in the carrots and onion. Toss the apples in the orange juice and add to the cabbages together with any remaining orange juice, and the celery, sweetcorn and raisins. Mix well.

For the dressing, mix the yogurt, parsley, and pepper to taste, in a bowl then pour over the cabbage mixture. Stir and serve.

Chinese-style Gingered Vegetables

serves 2

1 tbsp sunflower or groundnut oil

2.5-cm/1-inch piece fresh root ginger, peeled and grated

1 onion, thinly sliced

115 g/4 oz frozen French beans, cut into small pieces

450 g/1 lb bag frozen mixed vegetables

150 ml/5 fl oz water

2 heaped tbsp dark brown sugar

2 tbsp cornflour

4 tbsp malt vinegar

4 tbsp soy sauce

1 tsp ground ginger

Heat the oil in a wok or large frying pan, add the grated ginger and fry for 1 minute. Remove from the wok or pan and drain on kitchen paper.

Reduce the heat slightly and add the vegetables and water to the wok.

Cover with a lid or foil and cook for 5–6 minutes, or until the vegetables are tender.

Mix the sugar, cornflour, malt vinegar, soy sauce and ground ginger together in a bowl. Increase the heat to medium and add the mixture to the vegetables in the wok. Simmer for 1 minute, stirring, until thickened.

Return the ginger to the wok and stir to mix well. Heat through for 2 minutes and then serve immediately.

Crispy Roast Asparagus

serves 4

450 g/1 lb asparagus spears

2 tbsp extra virgin olive oil

1 tsp coarse sea salt

1 tbsp grated Parmesan-style vegetarian cheese, to serve

Preheat the oven to 200°C/400°F/Gas Mark 6.

Choose asparagus spears of similar widths. Trim the base of the spears so that all the stems are approximately the same length.

Arrange the asparagus in a single layer on a metal baking sheet. Drizzle with olive oil and sprinkle with salt.

Place the tray in the oven and bake for 10–15 minutes, turning once. Remove from the oven, transfer to an attractive dish and serve immediately, sprinkled with the grated cheese.

Hot Roast Peppers

serves 6

6 red peppers, deseeded and cut into thick strips

140 g/5 oz fresh green serrano or jalapeño chillies, deseeded and sliced into thin strips

2 garlic cloves, crushed

4 tbsp extra virgin olive oil

Preheat the oven to 200°C/400°F/Gas Mark 6. Put the peppers, chillies and garlic in a shallow casserole dish. Pour in the oil.

Cover and bake for 50–60 minutes, or until the peppers have softened. Remove the lid and reduce the temperature to 180°C/350°F/Gas Mark 4. Return the casserole dish to the oven and bake for a further 45 minutes, or until the peppers are very soft and beginning to char.

Serve immediately if serving hot. Alternatively, leave to cool, then transfer to a large screw-top jar and store in the refrigerator for up to 3 weeks, topped up with more olive oil to keep the peppers covered, if necessary.

Mexican Rice

serves 4

1 onion, chopped

400 g/14 oz plum tomatoes, peeled, deseeded and chopped

250 ml/9 fl oz vegetable stock

200 g/7 oz long-grain rice

salt and pepper

Put the onion and tomatoes in a food processor and process to a smooth purée. Scrape the purée into a saucepan, pour in the stock and bring to the boil over a medium heat, stirring occasionally.

Add the rice and stir once, then reduce the heat, cover and simmer for 20–25 minutes until all the liquid has been absorbed and the rice is tender. Season to taste with salt and pepper and serve immediately.

Spiced Lentils with Spinach

serves 4–6

2 tbsp olive oil

1 large onion, finely chopped

1 large garlic clove, crushed

½ tbsp ground cumin

½ tsp ground ginger

250 g/9 oz Puy lentils

about 600 ml/1 pint vegetable stock

100 g/3½ oz baby spinach leaves

2 tbsp fresh mint leaves

1 tbsp fresh coriander leaves

1 tbsp fresh flat-leaf parsley

lemon juice

salt and pepper

strips of lemon rind, to garnish

Heat the oil in a large frying pan over a medium heat. Add the onion and cook, stirring occasionally, for about 6 minutes. Stir in the garlic, cumin and ginger and cook, stirring occasionally, until the onion starts to brown.

Stir in the lentils. Pour in enough stock to cover the lentils by 2.5 cm/1 inch and bring to the boil. Lower the heat and simmer for 20–30 minutes until the lentils are tender.

Meanwhile, rinse the spinach leaves in several changes of cold water and shake dry. Finely chop the mint, coriander leaves and parsley.

If there isn't any stock left in the pan, add a little extra. Add the spinach and stir through until it just wilts. Stir in the mint, coriander and parsley. Adjust the seasoning, adding lemon juice and salt and pepper. Transfer to a serving bowl and serve, garnished with lemon rind.

Herby Potatoes & Onion

serves 4

900 g/2 lb waxy potatoes, cut into cubes

125 g/4½ oz butter

1 red onion, cut into 8 wedges

2 garlic cloves, crushed

1 tsp lemon juice

2 tbsp chopped fresh thyme

salt and pepper

Cook the cubed potatoes in a saucepan of boiling salted water for 10 minutes. Drain thoroughly.

Melt the butter in a large, heavy-based frying pan and add the red onion wedges, garlic and lemon juice. Cook, stirring constantly for 2–3 minutes.

Add the potatoes to the pan and mix well to coat in the butter mixture.

Reduce the heat, cover and cook for 25–30 minutes, or until the potatoes are golden brown and tender.

Sprinkle the chopped thyme over the top of the potatoes and season to taste with salt and pepper.

Transfer to a warm serving dish and serve immediately.

Colcannon

serves 4

225 g/8 oz green cabbage, shredded

5 tbsp milk

225 g/8 oz floury potatoes, diced

1 large leek, chopped

pinch of freshly grated nutmeg

1 tbsp butter, melted

salt and pepper

Cook the shredded cabbage in a saucepan of boiling salted water for 7–10 minutes. Drain thoroughly and set aside.

Meanwhile, in a separate saucepan, bring the milk to the boil and add the potatoes and leek. Reduce the heat and simmer for 15–20 minutes, or until they are cooked through.

Remove from the heat, stir in the freshly grated nutmeg and thoroughly mash the potatoes and leek together.

Add the drained cabbage to the mashed potato and leek mixture, season to taste and mix together well.

Spoon the mixture into a warmed serving dish, making a hollow in the centre with the back of a spoon.

Pour the melted butter into the hollow and serve the colcannon at once, while it is still hot.

Potatoes Dauphinois

serves 4

1 tbsp butter

675 g/1½ lb waxy potatoes,
sliced

2 garlic cloves, crushed

1 red onion, sliced

85 g/3 oz Gruyère-style
vegetarian cheese, grated

salt and pepper

300 ml/½ pint double
cream

Lightly grease a 1-litre/1¾-pint shallow ovenproof dish with butter.

Arrange a single layer of potato slices in the base of the prepared dish.

Top the potato slices with half the garlic, half the sliced red onion and one third of the grated cheese. Season to taste with a little salt and some pepper.

Repeat the layers in exactly the same order, finishing with a layer of potatoes topped with grated cheese.

Pour the cream over the top of the potatoes and cook in a preheated oven, 180°C/350°F/Gas Mark 4, for 1½ hours, or until the potatoes are cooked through and the top is browned and crispy. Serve the potatoes at once, straight from the dish.

Garlic Mash

serves 4

900 g/2 lb floury potatoes, cut into chunks

8 garlic cloves, crushed

150 ml/5 fl oz milk

85 g/3 oz butter

pinch of freshly grated nutmeg

salt and pepper

1 tbsp chopped fresh flat-leaf parsley, to garnish

Put the potatoes in a large saucepan. Add enough cold water to cover and a pinch of salt. Bring to the boil and cook for 10 minutes. Add the garlic and cook for 10 minutes more, until the potatoes are tender.

Drain the potatoes and garlic thoroughly, reserving 3 tablespoons of the cooking liquid.

Return the reserved liquid to the pan, add the milk and bring to simmering point. Add the butter and return the potatoes and garlic to the pan. Mash thoroughly with a potato masher.

Season to taste with nutmeg, salt and pepper and beat the potato mixture with a wooden spoon until light and fluffy. Garnish with flat-leaf parsley and serve immediately.

Pesto Potatoes

serves 4

900 g/2 lb small new potatoes

75 g/2¾ oz fresh basil

2 tbsp pine kernels

3 garlic cloves, crushed

100 ml/3½ fl oz olive oil

75 g/2¾ oz mixed Parmesan-style and pecorino-style vegetarian cheeses, grated

salt and pepper

fresh basil sprigs, to garnish

Cook the potatoes in a saucepan of boiling salted water for 15 minutes or until tender. Drain well, transfer to a warm serving dish and keep warm until required.

Meanwhile, put the fresh basil, pine kernels, crushed garlic and a little salt and pepper to taste in a food processor. Blend for 30 seconds, adding the oil gradually, until smooth.

Remove the mixture from the food processor and transfer it to a mixing bowl. Stir in the grated cheeses.

Spoon the pesto sauce over the potatoes and mix well. Garnish with fresh basil sprigs and serve immediately.

Steamed Vegetables Parcels

serves 4

115 g/4 oz French beans

55 g/2 oz mangetouts

12 baby carrots

8 baby onions or shallots

12 baby turnips

8 radishes

55 g/2 oz unsalted butter or margarine

4 thinly pared strips of lemon rind

4 tsp finely chopped fresh chervil

4 tbsp dry white wine

salt and pepper

Cut out 4 double thickness rounds of greaseproof paper about 30 cm/12 inches in diameter.

Divide the French beans, mangetouts, carrots, onions or shallots, turnips and radishes among the rounds, placing them on one half. Season to taste with salt and pepper and dot with the butter. Add a strip of lemon rind to each. Sprinkle with the chervil and drizzle with the wine. Fold over the double layer of paper, twisting the edges together to seal.

Bring a large pan of water to the boil and place a steamer on top. Put the parcels in the steamer, cover tightly and steam for 8–10 minutes. Serve the parcels immediately, to be unwrapped at table.

Peas with Baby Onions

serves 4

15 g/½ oz unsalted butter

175 g/6 oz baby onions

900 g/2 lb fresh peas, shelled

125 ml/4 fl oz water

2 tbsp plain flour

150 ml/5 fl oz double cream

1 tbsp chopped fresh parsley

1 tbsp lemon juice

salt and pepper

Melt the butter in a large, heavy-based saucepan. Add the whole baby onions and cook, stirring occasionally, for 5 minutes. Add the peas and cook, stirring constantly, for a further 3 minutes, then add the measured water and bring to the boil. Lower the heat, partially cover and simmer for 10 minutes.

Beat the flour into the cream. Remove the pan from the heat and stir in the cream mixture and parsley and season to taste with salt and pepper.

Return the pan to the heat and cook, stirring gently but constantly, for about 3 minutes, until thickened.

Stir the lemon juice into the sauce and serve the peas immediately.

Chinese Vegetables

serves 4

2 tbsp groundnut oil

350 g/12 oz broccoli florets

1 tbsp chopped fresh root ginger

2 onions, cut into 8 pieces

3 celery sticks, sliced

175 g/6 oz baby spinach

125 g/4½ oz mangetouts

6 spring onions, quartered

2 garlic cloves, crushed

2 tbsp light soy sauce

2 tsp caster sugar

2 tbsp dry sherry

1 tbsp hoisin sauce

150 ml/5 fl oz vegetable stock

Heat the groundnut oil in a preheated wok until it is almost smoking.

Add the broccoli florets, chopped root ginger, onions and celery to the wok and stir-fry for 1 minute.

Add the spinach, mangetouts, spring onions and garlic and stir-fry for 3–4 minutes.

Mix together the soy sauce, caster sugar, sherry, hoisin sauce and vegetable stock.

Pour the stock mixture into the wok, mixing well to coat the vegetables.

Cover the wok and cook over a medium heat for 2–3 minutes, or until the vegetables are cooked through, but still crisp.

Transfer the Chinese fried vegetables to a warm serving dish and serve immediately.

Chargrilled Vegetables

serves 6

2 sweet potatoes, sliced

3 courgettes, halved lengthways

3 red peppers, deseeded and cut into quarters

olive oil, for brushing

salt

for the salsa verde

2 fresh green chillies, halved and deseeded

8 spring onions, roughly chopped

2 garlic cloves, roughly chopped

1 tbsp capers

bunch of fresh parsley, roughly chopped

grated rind and juice of 1 lime

4 tbsp lemon juice

6 tbsp olive oil

1 tbsp green Tabasco sauce

pepper

Cook the sweet potato slices in boiling water for 5 minutes. Drain and set aside to cool. Sprinkle the courgettes with salt and set aside for 30 minutes. Rinse and pat dry with kitchen paper.

Meanwhile, make the salsa verde. Put the chillies, spring onions and garlic in a food processor and process briefly. Add the capers and parsley and pulse until finely chopped. Transfer the mixture to a serving bowl.

Stir in the lime rind and juice, lemon juice, olive oil and Tabasco. Season to taste with pepper, cover with clingfilm and chill in the refrigerator until required.

Brush the sweet potato slices, courgettes and peppers with olive oil and spread out on a grill rack or barbecue. Grill, turning once and brushing with more olive oil, for 8–10 minutes, until tender and lightly charred. Serve the vegetables immediately with the salsa verde.

Lemon Beans

serves 4

900 g/2 lb mixed green
beans, such as broad
beans, French beans,
runner beans

75 g/2½ oz butter or
margarine

4 tsp plain flour

300 ml/½ pint vegetable
stock

5 tbsp dry white wine

6 tbsp single cream

3 tbsp chopped fresh mixed
herbs

grated rind of 1 lemon

2 tbsp lemon juice

salt and pepper

Cook the beans in a saucepan of boiling salted water for
10 minutes, or until tender. Drain and place in a warmed
serving dish.

Meanwhile, melt the butter in a saucepan. Add the flour and
cook, stirring constantly, for 1 minute. Remove the pan from
the heat and gradually stir in the stock and wine. Return the
pan to the heat and bring to the boil, stirring.

Remove the pan from the heat once again and stir in the
single cream, mixed herbs, lemon rind and juice. Season
with salt and pepper to taste. Pour the sauce over the
beans, mixing well to coat thoroughly. Serve immediately.